Love stories

of GREAT MISSIONARIES

Mini-Reviews

"Engaging and moving! To read again of the sacrifices these men and women were willing to suffer for the cause of Christ made me wonder again how much I'm willing to sacrifice."
—*Roger, a pastor*

"The introduction is relevant to those of us who are not missionaries. I appreciated the clarity of the Gospel message—the very reason these missionaries suffered and gave up so much. I am encouraged in ministering to my husband!"
—*Abbe, a wife and mother*

"These couples did not wear rose colored glasses. They knew and accepted the brutal, unromantic future God had laid out for them.... In all of these stories I felt a connection. The longings, frustrations and difficulties they had are not foreign to the average believer."
—*Shawn, a mother and artist*

"The section on the surrender and service of godly women is remarkable, but I was struck by the overwhelming need for God to work through men! It is a great and needed read for all ages, but especially Millennials as they mature into their thirties."
—*Kyle, a pastor*

"What a read! The introduction and afterword are excellent additions that would be helpful in preparing future students for the mission field."
—*Deb, a retired medical missionary*

Mini-Reviews

"Enjoyable and timely, fresh and relevant in this now globalized and connected world. The book highlights some of the most intimate targets that the enemy exploits in our relationships."
—*Jeremy, a surgeon and missions mobilizer*

"I was challenged and inspired to continue to work on a closer relationship with my boys and use my influence wisely in support of their faith and future marriages."
—*Migena, a mom*

"For family devotions we are always looking for missionary biographies like this, ones that speak to the heart and are good for older kids and teens."
—*Curt, a pastor and college professor*

"As parents it was an encouragement and challenge to us to raise and nurture our sweet boys to serve Him—and then be ready to let them go whenever and wherever He sees fit to call them."
—*Jessica, a pastor's wife*

"I absolutely loved this little book. Every bit of it."
—*Laura, a mother of missionaries*

"A blessing and very strengthening. The freshness of it was stimulating for my soul. These stories are representative: they could be repeated a thousand times, especially in the past but even now."
—*Matt, a missionary*

SAILING OF JUDSON AND HIS BRIDE
on the *Caravan* from Salem, Massachusetts
February 19, 1812

Love stories

of Great Missionaries

Adoniram & Ann Judson
Robert & Mary Moffat
David & Mary Livingstone
James & Emily Gilmour
François & Christina Coillard
Henry Martyn & Lydia Grenfell

Belle Marvel Brain

adapted, with afterword, by David Hosaflook

Love Stories of Great Missionaries: Adoniram and Ann Judson, Robert and Mary Moffat, David and Mary Livingstone, James and Emily Gilmour, François and Christina Coillard, Henry Martyn and Lydia Grenfell

Originally published in 1913 (Fleming H. Revell)

Adapted text, introduction, and afterword © David Hosaflook, 2021

ISBN 978-1-946244-96-3

IAPS (Longwood, FL)

Publishers-in-Publication Data:

Name: Brain, Belle Marvel; Hosaflook, David (editor)

Title: Love Stories of Great Missionaries: Adoniram and Ann Judson, Robert and Mary Moffat, David and Mary Livingstone, James and Emily Gilmour, François and Christina Coillard, Henry Martyn and Lydia Grenfell

ISBN 978-1-946244-96-3 (paperback)
ISBN 978-1-946244-97-0 (e-book)

Subjects (BISAC): REL045000 RELIGION / Christian Ministry / Missions | REL012050 RELIGION / Christian Living / Love & Marriage | BIO018000 BIOGRAPHY & AUTOBIOGRAPHY / Religious

DEDICATIONS
(OLD & NEW)

1913

*To the girl who is tempted to say "No"
to her beloved because
he is a missionary volunteer*

2021

*To the girl who did not say "No,"
with my love and gratitude for enduring
much hardship—for Him—with me*

CONTENTS

INTRODUCTION

David Hosaflook, missionary

This little gem of a book is about men and women whose mission was to tell others about the greatest Love Story of all, the Gospel—the Story of how God loved the fallen and condemned people of Earth and gave His only Son to come down to them, teach them, and rescue them (John 3:16).

This Son, made human in order to die and remaining divine in order to save, shed His blood in death so that the world might live. The Bible describes this as being both excruciatingly painful and eternally joyful for Him. Then He proved his authority and power by rising from the dead. On the basis of that fervent act, God offers a free gift—*eternal life*—to all those who will turn away from the sin that keeps them condemned and believe on the Son who can set them free.

Missionaries get to tell this amazing Love Story to people who have never heard it. They are God's runners and heralds.

The work of missionaries, however, is less romantic and more complicated than the previous paragraph suggests. This is because the Gospel is not only a love story, but also a war story. It aims to expose sin, expel darkness, and destroy death. It claims there is *only one* God (not many or none) and *only one* mediator-Messiah, Jesus Christ. This claim is threatening to other faiths and non-faiths, especially to religious systems entrenched within delicate and inter-dependent political, economic, and social structures. Paul the Apostle witnessed this when his preaching at Ephesus threatened the idols industry and the silversmiths initiated an uproar (Acts 19).

Even today, when people hear the Gospel (or when missionaries merely *attempt* to tell them about it), they react unpredictably, often with antagonism. Since missionaries are the ones proclaiming the authority of King Jesus, it is the missionaries who usually bear the brunt of the counter-attacks unleashed against Him.

In addition to spiritual conflicts, missionaries also face physical obstacles: distance to be traveled, unwritten languages to learn and encode, cultural dissonance to navigate, and manifold hardships to endure. This was especially true from the 1700s to early 1900s, when saying "good-bye" cost more than it does now. Missionaries sailed to their destinations with little thought of return. Communicating home by letter took many weeks or months. When missionaries died prematurely from disease or persecution, their loved ones were sad, but not surprised.

The missionaries whose love stories are told in this little book are part of a truly great generation. Their names are eminently recognizable in British, American, and French Christianity. They did not consider themselves great, but rather as ordinary men and women who felt fear, pain, fatigue, and loneliness like everyone else. They relied on Christ's strength in their weakness. Let us consider what the call to missions meant to them.

For this I call your attention to two single missionaries without the name recognition of a Judson or a Hudson: *Levi Parsons* and *Pliny Fisk*—the first two American missionaries in the Ottoman Empire. In 1819 they set off together for Jerusalem. In their farewell sermons at Park Street Church in Boston, Mr. Parsons preached from an optimistic text prophesying that "the children of Israel shall return and seek the Lord their God ... in the latter days" (Hosea 3:4–5). Mr. Fisk, on the other hand, preached from a more sobering text, Acts 20, in which Paul stated that he (like them) was going to Jerusalem, but believed that in every city, imprisonment and afflictions awaited him. There was space in their theology and missiology for this dialectical co-existence: a desire for mass conversions and a simultaneous recognition that their preaching might fall on deaf ears. Jesus himself, after all, had spoken of a narrow path and was crucified. The prophet Jeremiah was instructed to preach even though he was forewarned that no one would believe him. Mass rejection and early death, then, were two of the potential scenarios missionaries expected. Parsons ended up dying in 1822 in Alexandria, not three years after his optimistic sermon in Boston; whereas Fisk died in 1825 in Beirut.

Imagine your feelings, ladies, if in the 1800s, an idealistic young man had asked you to join with him in marriage and mission. Belle Marvel Brain dedicates these stories to you, hoping you would not say "no" based on a preference to live more comfortably and safely in your earthly homeland.

Now imagine being Ann Hasseltine's daddy, opening Adoniram Judson's famous letter asking him to part with his daughter forever, telling him she will surely suffer want, distress, degradation, insult, persecution, and perhaps a violent death. Agreeing to this boy (remember, he was not *yet* a "great missionary") must have felt like plunging the first shovel into his daughter's burial plot and into his own heart. The Hasseltines' consent makes me want to read more about their faith and parenting!

I have republished this little book (with light adaptations) because I find it delightful and worthy of rediscovery. It is more than a hundred years old and contains terminology and traditions today's reader might find entertainingly odd, but the stories are surprisingly refreshing and relevant, especially to missions-loving Christians, singles contemplating love and marriage, parents of missionaries, young people, mid-life missionaries struggling to care for both family and flock, and veteran missionaries who have served with their spouses for decades.

A forewarning: Belle Brain (1859–1933) writes passionately to her generation. She can be dogmatic, even critical. If she sounds old-fashioned, it is because she is, well, old-fashioned. But sometimes we need older writings like hers as a check and balance to the worldly relativism that bombards our minds continually and has seeped subversively into the church.

In my afterword, I probe some questions likely to be raised and offer perspectives as a man with both single and married missionary experience. So as you read, do not get sidetracked by questions, extrapolations, or objections—just file them away and we will debrief together at the end.

For now, just enjoy these chapters for what they are: beautiful and entertaining love stories of missionaries who had first fallen in love with Jesus Christ and the Love Story He gave to the world.

FOREWORD

Belle Marvel Brain, 1913

A source that remains anonymous related this story, related to the call to foreign missions:

> At the Ohio State Christian Endeavor Convention held in Zanesville in 1912, it was the privilege of the writer to conduct the conferences on the work of the missionary committee. At one of these, after stating the causes that had led a number of great missionaries to the field, the young people were asked to tell what had given them their own interest in missions. Many life stories were told and a deep impression was made.

> That evening, in personal conversation with the writer, a prominent minister who had been present at the conference in the afternoon, confessed that he had expected to be a missionary but that his fiancée (at that time his wife) was unwilling to go and he had given it up for her sake. Next

morning another prominent minister made the same statement.

What did it mean? Here were two pastors, both highly successful in their work, lost to the foreign field because being a missionary would have interfered with their human affections.

Were there others who had rejected the call for like reasons? I dare say there are a multitude of them!

Investigation has proved what every mission board secretary knows, to his sorrow, that many a young volunteer, pledged to foreign missions, turns aside from his life-work because of some affair of love. The call of Love, clashing with the call of God, proves the stronger. Yet, perchance Love's call was of God as much as the call to the field, and through faith, patience, and prayer, might have been brought into harmony with it.

It was in the hope of helping young people to solve aright the problem of marriage and missions that these love stories of great missionaries were searched out and written. Last year they found publication in the columns of *The Sunday School Times*. Now, through the courtesy and kindness of the editors of *The Times*, they form the chapters of this little book. May God grant they be blessed as they go forth on their mission again.

It must not be imagined that these love stories are the only ones in the history of missions worth telling! There are others just as heroic. These were selected because each represents a different type and impresses a much needed lesson.

BELLE M. BRAIN
Schenectady, New York

ADONIRAM JUDSON
Ann Hasseltine

Winning a Wife in the Homeland

The first time Adoniram Judson saw Ann Hasseltine his whole heart went out to her. It was a genuine case of love at first sight.

And no wonder. It was not surprising that a young man like Adoniram would be drawn to her. Tall and slender, with dark eyes and curling hair, and a bright, vivacious manner, she was not only beautiful, but had the added charms of a keen and well developed mind, and a spirit as dauntless and devout as Judson's own.

It was during the sessions of the Massachusetts General Association of Congregational Churches held in Bradford in June, 1810—that historic meeting at which the American Board of Commissioners for Foreign Missions (ABCFM) was born—that the two first met. Ann lived in Bradford, and Adoniram had come, in company with "the three Samuels," Newell, Nott, and Mills, to present a paper to the Association stating their desire to become missionaries, and asking if they might expect support from the American churches.

The story of their first meeting is told by Judson's son:

> During the sessions the ministers gathered for a dinner beneath Mr. Hasseltine's hospitable roof. His youngest daughter, Ann, was waiting on the table. Her attention was attracted to the young student whose bold missionary projects were making such a stir. But what was her surprise to observe, as she moved about the table, that he seemed completely absorbed in his plate! Little did she dream that she had already woven her spell about his young heart, and that he was, at that very time, composing a graceful stanza in her praise!

An introduction followed, and before long Judson asked her if she would be his wife and go with him to carry the gospel to the unreached peoples of India.

It was a momentous question, which she did not answer at once. In every way he was the kind of man she would choose. Slender and refined-looking,

with dark eyes and chestnut hair much like her own, the son of a highly respected New England minister, and first honors man at Brown in 1807, any young woman might have been proud to be offered his hand, and Ann returned his affection. Had he been content to stay in America and serve the "biggest church in Boston" (whose minister wanted him for a colleague), it would not have taken her long to decide.

But to go with him to India? That was another question.

It is hard to realize in our day what it meant to be a missionary then. No one had as yet left America to carry the Gospel to India, and public opinion was against it. For a man it was regarded as absurd; for a woman, "entirely inconsistent with prudence and delicacy." The voyage was long and perilous, the climate of India unfavorable, and the danger of violent death at the hands of the natives believed to be great. Then, too, the mission was for life, with no provision for furlough.

No wonder Ann hesitated. It does not cost quite so much to be a missionary in these days, yet many a young woman, when asked the question that Adoniram asked Ann, even though her heart prompts an affirmative answer, either rejects the suit of her beloved, or uses all her powers of persuasion to induce him to remain in the homeland with her.

Not so Ann Hasseltine.

Though the idea appalled her, she bravely faced it and sought to know whether it was really God's call. Most of her friends were violently opposed to her going, and of the few to whom she turned for advice, only two or three gave her any encouragement whatever.

Though Judson's whole heart was set on her going, he made no effort to bias her decision by minimizing the dangers or throwing a false glamour of romance over the future, but appealed instead to her love for Christ and the rewards promised to those who serve Him. When at length she said something about the consent of parents, he wrote to her father as follows:

I have now to ask whether you can consent to part with your daughter early next spring, to see her no more in this world? Whether you can consent to her departure to a heathen land, and the hardships and sufferings of a missionary life? Whether you can consent to her exposure to the dangers of the ocean; to the fatal influence of the southern climate of India; to every kind of want and distress; to degradation, insult, persecution, and perhaps a violent death? Can you consent to all this for the sake of Him who left His heavenly home and died for her and for you; for the sake of perishing and immortal souls; for the sake of Zion and the glory of God? Can you consent to all this in the hope of soon meeting your daughter in the world of glory, with a crown of righteousness brightened by the acclamations of praise which shall redound to her Saviour from heathen saved, through her means, from eternal woe and despair?

It was an honest and honorable letter, though scarcely adapted, in the eyes of the world, to gaining its end. Few fathers would consent to a daughter entering upon such a career. But the spirit of obedience to the divine will was as strong in Mr. Hasseltine's heart as in that of Ann and her beloved. If God wanted his daughter, dear though she was to him, he would not withhold her.

And so they were betrothed—the earnest young student volunteer of twenty-two who had already done so much for missions, and the fair girl of twenty-one to whom belongs the honor of being the first American woman to decide to go as a missionary to the unevangelized people of Asia. Be it not thought this decision was made merely because of her love for young Judson. In a letter to a trusted girlfriend, dated September 8, 1810, she thus states her motives:

> I have ever made you a confidant. I will still confide in you, and beg for your prayers, that I may be directed in regard to this subject I shall communicate.
>
> I feel willing and expect, if nothing in providence prevents, to spend my days in this world in heathen lands. Yes, Lydia, I have about come to the determination to give up all my comforts and enjoyments here, sacrifice my affection to relatives and friends, and go where God, in his providence, shall see fit to place me. My determinations are not hasty or formed without viewing the dangers, trials, and hardships attendant on a missionary life. Nor were my determinations formed in consequence of an attachment to an earthly object; but with a sense of my obligation to God, and a full conviction of its being a call in providence, and consequently my duty. My feelings have been exquisite in regard to the subject. Now my mind is settled and composed, and is willing to leave the event with God—none can support one under trials and afflictions but

Him. In Him alone I feel a disposition to confide.
How short is time, how boundless is eternity! If
we may be considered worthy to suffer for Jesus
here, will it not enhance our happiness hereaf-
ter? Pray for me. Spend whole evenings in prayer
for those who go to carry the gospel to the poor
heathen.

It must have been rather a solemn affair, this
courtship of Adoniram and Ann. It could not be
otherwise with the Puritan spirit still so strong in
New England. At that time, and indeed for long
after, levity was considered most unbecoming in
a missionary, and the fitness of a candidate who
indulged in much laughter was seriously questioned.
Yet neither Ann nor Adoniram was by nature seri-
ous and sober. Up to the time of her conversion in
her seventeenth year, Ann had been playful and
carefree, delighting in an endless round of parties
and regarding herself as entirely too old to say her
prayers! And Adoniram, becoming tainted with
French infidelity through association with a carefree and witty college chum, had started out to see
the world, and while seeing it had fallen in with a
band of roaming players, whose wild and vagabond
life he shared for a time.

But now Adoniram and Ann were as devout and
as discreet as anyone could wish. Of the frequent
letters that passed between them, the three that

have been given to the public—letters of Adoniram to Ann, dated respectively December 30 and 31, 1810, and January 1, 1811—show a complete consecration to God. That of New Year's Day pictures in such realistic terms the sorrows that may overtake them during the year that it is a wonder Ann did not break the engagement at once! But it breathes a spirit of true love for her, and is not without its playful touch. Longing to be united to her and eager to begin his great work, he expresses the wish that this may be the year in which she will change her name and they will cross the ocean and dwell in heathen lands together.

Not until the following year were these wishes fulfilled. On September 11, 1811, Messrs. Judson, Hall, Newell, and Nott (Luther Rice was later added to the number) received their appointment as missionaries from the Board, but as opportunities for obtaining passage to India were of rare occurrence in those days, no time was set for their departure.

At length the way unexpectedly opened. In January, 1812, it was found that two ships were about to sail for Calcutta, the *Harmony* from Philadelphia and the *Caravan* from Salem, and that by dividing the missionaries into two parties, passage could be secured for them all.

The time was short and there were many preparations to make, but at length all was ready. On February 5 there was a quiet wedding at Bradford, and an agonizing parting, as Ann and Adoniram Judson went forth, expecting never more to return. The next day, at a solemn and affecting service held in the old Tabernacle Church at Salem, where a picture of the scene and the settee on which they sat are still preserved, Judson and his colleagues received ordination.

Then, on February 19, after an unexpected delay of some days, the Judsons, in company with Samuel and Harriet Newell, boarded the *Caravan* and began their wedding journey to the field.

It was well they had counted the cost. The trials in store for them, though of a somewhat different nature than they had anticipated, were fully as great. Contrary to all expectation, the ocean voyage was completed without disaster; neither of them met with a violent death at the hands of the heathen; and each, in the good providence of God, was permitted to return once to the homeland.

But expulsion from India, the separation from their colleagues, the odium cast on their names resulting from their change of belief in regard to the method of baptism, their settlement in Burma (a land they had been led to regard with feelings of horror), and the twenty-one months' imprisonment at Ava and Oung-pen-la—these were things they had not even dreamed of.

But, though God permitted them to suffer so sorely, He gave them abundant success.

Many notable men and women have gone out since from America, but the service of these two has not yet been surpassed—perhaps not even equaled. In that dark land they dreaded to enter, Judson planted one of the most famous and successful of missions, and his wife proved herself one of the world's greatest heroines. The change in denomination that cost them so sore resulted in the forming of a second great missionary society in America— the society so long known as the American Baptist Missionary Union—and the accounts of their sufferings at Ava kindled fires of heroic self-sacrifice that have never died out.

God evidently made no mistake when He gave Ann Hasseltine to Adoniram Judson to be his wedded wife. Without her at his side to cheer and comfort and help him, it would have been hard to plant the mission in Burma, and seemingly impossible for him to have endured the tortures at Ava.

ROBERT MOFFAT
Mary Smith

A Case of Parental Objection

Not long after Robert Moffat entered the service of James Smith, of the Dukinfield Nurseries, he fell in love with his employer's only daughter.

Mr. Smith had been afraid this might happen. While returning home one day from Manchester, he had promised his friend, the Rev. William Roby, to take Moffat—the young Scotch gardener who felt called of God to be a missionary—into his employ. On that eventful day, it occurred to Smith that perhaps it would cost him his daughter.

But Rev. Roby was so anxious to have his young protégé near him, and there had been no other opening. Besides, James Smith liked the young man and thought he would make a good workman.

Perhaps there was no ground for his fears, after all. The young man had been obliged to give up his plans, at least for the present. The London Society to whom Moffat had offered himself, through Roby, had declined to accept him. There were so many applicants that only the best could be sent, and young Moffat had had little schooling.

End as it might, James Smith had given his word, and he would stand by it. So, about New Year's, 1816, Robert Moffat began work at the Dukinfield Nurseries.

Very soon he made the acquaintance of his master's young daughter. Beautiful in face, polished in manners, and the expectant of a considerable fortune, she was attractive enough to win the heart of any young man. To her father's new assistant, however, she had the added charm of an interest in missions as deep as his own. Her education in a Moravian school had laid the foundations; and two years before, at a meeting in Manchester, she had been so deeply impressed with the needs of the heathen that she had sent up a silent petition to God that some time she might be permitted to work in South Africa.

From the outset, Robert Moffat and Mary Smith were attracted to one another. Ere long they became

so deeply attached that they plighted their troth one to another.

For a time the course of their true love ran smooth. But by and by there was trouble. Through the intervention of Mr. Roby, the directors in London were induced to reconsider their decision, and bade the young Scotchman be ready to sail within a few months. He was assigned at first to the South Seas with John Williams. But presently, deeming "*thae twa lads ower young to gang togeither*" (Moffat was twenty-one and Williams twenty)—this was changed to South Africa. Thus strangely was God preparing to answer Mary Smith's prayer.

To Robert's parents in Scotland, his going was a trial of no common sort. Yet they did nothing to hinder, but bade him "Godspeed." The old father wrote, with dignified resignation, that whatever might be his own feelings or those of Robert's mother, they "dared not oppose his design, lest haply in so doing they should be found fighting with God."

Not so Mary Smith's parents! Both were deeply pious, and ardent promoters of missions. Yet they declared they could not relinquish their daughter and refused to give their consent.

Poor young Moffat! He had not realized that his going might cost him so much. But his life had been laid on God's altar, and he would not withdraw it. Nor did Mary Smith ask it. The idea of a separation appalled them, but their happiness must not interfere with God's work. So Robert prepared to go out alone.

By and by a letter came from the directors that made it still harder. "All candidates are expected to take partners along with them," it said. This was a new sorrow that cost Mary Smith many tears. Yet she offered to release Robert from his engagement, and let him choose another to go in her place. But to him this seemed little short of a crime. How could he offer his hand to another when his heart was still in Mary Smith's keeping? Yet if God willed it, he must obey.

But God did not ask this sacrifice of him. "From the clearest indications of His Providence, He bids me go out alone," he wrote to his parents, after long hours of prayer; "and He who appoints crosses and disappointments also imparts resignation and grace sufficient unto the day. So I am bold to adopt the language of Eli, and to say, 'It is the Lord, let Him do what seemeth Him good.'"

And so it was settled. The directors acquiesced in the decision, and on October 18, 1816, when Moffat sailed for South Africa, leaving his heart in old England, no new tie had been formed to separate him from his loved one, and there was nothing to prevent his claiming his own tie, should her parents ever be willing to surrender her to him. Sore as was their sorrow at parting, the young lovers thanked God for this.

Moffat's destination in Africa was Africaner's kraal, in Namaqualand, beyond the confines of Cape Colony, where the Ebners were working. Africaner was the terror of the whole region, and all along the way from Cape Town, the young missionary heard dire predictions of the fate that awaited him. "One warned me that he would set me up for a mark for his boys to shoot at," he says. "Another, that he would strip off my skin and make a drum of it to dance to; another, that he would make a drinking cup of my skull. One kind, motherly lady, wiping the tears from her eyes, bade me farewell, saying, 'Had you been an old man it would have been nothing, for you would soon have died, whether or no; but you are young, and going to become a prey to that monster.'"

But when Moffat reached the kraal, Africaner seemed glad to see him and ordered his women to build him a house. In half an hour they had it all ready! It was a frail structure, in shape like a beehive, with a single opening large enough to crawl in, yet he lived in it nearly six months.

Africaner's heart was soon won and the work progressed fairly well, but life in the little hut was lonely and comfortless. Soon after Moffat arrived, the Ebners withdrew, leaving him alone, with no prospect of reinforcement. He rarely saw another foreigner, and for nearly a year did not hear a word spoken in English.

Great indeed was his need of Mary Smith's care. He wrote to his parents:

> I have many difficulties to encounter, being alone. No one can do anything for me in my household affairs. I must attend to everything, which hinders my work, for I could wish to have almost nothing to do but instruct the heathen. I am carpenter, smith, cooper, tailor, shoemaker, miller, baker, and housekeeper—the last the most burdensome. An old Namaqua woman milks my cow, makes a fire, and washes. All the other things I do myself, though I seldom prepare anything till impelled by hunger. I wish many times my mother saw me. My house is

always pretty clean, but oh, what a confusion among my linen!

During the long winter evenings at the old home in Scotland, his mother had taught her boys to knit and sew, while she told them thrilling stories of Moravian missions. Robert had sometimes rebelled, but now he was glad, for he had frequent need to make use of his needle.

Meanwhile Mary Smith's heart was breaking, far away in old England. She was sure God was calling her to Africa and was afraid she was doing wrong not to go. But her parents showed no signs of relenting. There was nothing to do but to wait and to pray, and these both the young people were doing. Thousands of miles lay between them, yet their prayers were ever ascending in united petition to heaven.

Their great solace was letters—long, loving letters that kept them in touch with each other. But on November 26, 1818, one came to Robert in Africa that he was disappointed to receive. In it his dear Mary told him, with deep sorrow of heart, that since her father declared he would never give his consent, she had at last relinquished all hope of coming to Africa. It well-nigh crushed him, yet in his sorrow he drew closer to God.

But God was merely testing the faith of His children. Their prayers had been heard after all!

Less than one month later, Mary's parents suddenly and unexpectedly gave their consent to her going!

"This is by no means what I expected a week ago," she wrote to Robert's parents. "Previous to the arrival of the last letters, my father persisted in saying I should never have his consent; and my dear mother has uniformly asserted that it would break her heart; nevertheless, they both yesterday calmly resigned me into the hands of the Lord, declaring they durst no longer withhold me."

When the news reached Robert in Africa he wrote to his parents at once:

> I have just received letters from Miss Smith. The whole scene is changed. I have now reason to believe that God will make her path plain to Africa. This, I trust, will be soon, for a missionary without a wife in this country is like a boat with one oar.

Mary Smith lost no time in preparing to go to her beloved. The wedding, of course, would take place in Africa. It was out of the question for Robert to come for his bride. It was a hard journey for a young girl to take all alone, and there was some delay in securing her passage; but at length, on September 7, 1819, she boarded the *British Colony* and sailed for the Cape in the care of a minister of the Dutch Church and his wife.

Be it not thought that her going cost her no sorrow. Eager as she was to be at work with Robert in Africa, the anguish of parting with father and mother and brothers was almost unbearable.

Meanwhile in Africa Robert was being put to another difficult test. Early in 1819, Dr. Philip and Mr. John Campbell arrived from London to inspect the various stations, and begged Moffat to make the tour with them. They needed his help, but it would take nearly a year and prevent his meeting his betrothed when she landed in Africa. Was it his duty to go? Could he allow strangers meet her, even though they were dear friends of his? But God had been good, and His work must be first. So he agreed to go. God accepted his spirit of sacrifice but did not exact its full payment. About midway in the journey war broke out with the Kaffirs, and the party had to turn back, bringing Moffat to Cape Town when the *British Colony* swung into port.

Their meeting was very affecting. Mary Smith wrote to her parents:

> My cup of happiness seems almost full. I have found my dear friend all that my heart could desire, except his being almost worn out with anxiety, and his very look makes my heart ache. Our worthy friend Melville met me on board and conducted me to his house, where a scene

took place such as I never wish to experience again. We have received each other from the Lord and are happy.

To this Robert adds in the same letter:

When the news of your beloved daughter's arrival reached me, it was to me nothing less than life from the dead. My prayers were answered, and the promises which had long been my refuge were fulfilled. Mary, my own dear Mary, is now far distant from you; but let this comfort you, that, although in a land of strangers, she is under the care of our ever-present God, and united to one who promises to be father, mother, and husband to her, and will never forget the sacrifice you have made in committing to his care your only daughter.

Three weeks later, on December 27, 1819, the long-deferred wedding took place in St. George's Church, Cape Town, Dr. Philip taking the place of the absent father, and the Melvilles opening their house for the feast. Shortly after, the young couple left in ox wagons for their wedding journey of six hundred miles to their field.

Such was the happy ending of the romance of the Moffats. Theirs was a union truly ideal. For more than fifty years they walked hand in hand, doing God's work with a zeal that has rarely been equaled.

Through it all Mary Moffat was the truest of helpmeets. "My father never would have been the missionary he was but for her care," says their son.

When God took her home, the sense of her loss overwhelmed her poor husband. "For fifty-three years I have had her to pray for me," was his first pitiful cry when he found she was gone. But what a precious gift of God she had been!

Robert and Mary Moffat
after more than fifty years in Africa

DAVID LIVINGSTONE
Mary Moffat

Finding a Wife on the Field

David Livingstone was fancy free when he sailed for Africa in 1840. He had opinions of his own on the subject of matrimony and missions, and no fair young girl crossing his path had as yet led him to change them.

The Directors of the London Missionary Society had asked him the usual questions when he applied to them two years before. One of them was in regard to his matrimonial prospects. In answering this he was very explicit. "I am not married," he said, "nor under any engagement of marriage, nor have I indeed been in love! I would prefer to go out unmarried, that I may, like the great apostle, be without family cares, and give myself entirely up to the work."

His interest at that time was centered in China, but the Opium War broke out and prevented his going. Just then Robert Moffat came home and won him for Africa. Good, motherly, wise Mary Moffat did all she could to persuade him to marry. She could not forget what her own Robert had suffered in Africa before her parents allowed her to go to him, and was loath to see another young man go out with such prospects. But Livingstone thought he knew best and declined to take her advice.

The first weeks in Africa did not change his opinion. He still thought he had done well to go out alone, with no wife to hamper his movements. To his friend Watt, a missionary in India, who, like himself, had elected to go out unmarried, he wrote, soon after landing:

> Mrs. Sewall writes that she believes you are heartily sorry you had not a helpmate with you. I have told her I am sure you are not. I am conscious myself that I am better without. All the missionaries' wives I have seen denounce my single blessedness in no measured terms. Some even insinuated that the reason I am thus is that I have been unable to get a spouse. But I put that down very speedily by assuming that it is a great deal easier for a missionary to get married in England than to come out single. In the latter case a vigorous resistance must be made, but in the former only yield up the affair into the

hands of any friend, and it is managed for you in a twinkling! This is a digression, but perhaps it may come in seasonably if your colleague's spouse is hard on you.

But bachelor life in Africa did not prove the ideal thing he had thought it. Often going weeks at a time with no fellowship with those of his own nation, he began to sense great loneliness; and being his own housekeeper, laundress, and seamstress was hard work and took up too much of his time. Besides, there was ministry for women and children that only a woman could do.

After three years of roughing it, he began to wonder if marrying was such a bad thing for a missionary after all. Perhaps, if he could find the right kind of wife, he might do it himself after all—not now, but some time far off in the future.

A letter from Watt put his mind on it harder than ever. From the "apologetic-for-marriage" strain in which it was written, Livingstone inferred that his friend was about to marry, and wrote him as follows:

> I hope you will be happy. Here there is no one worth taking off one's hat to. Daughters of missionaries have miserably contracted minds. Colonial ladies are worse. There's no outlet for me when I begin to think of getting married than that of sending home an advertisement for the Evangelical Magazine, and if I get old it must be for some decent sort of widow. In the meantime I am too busy to think of anything of the kind.

The next year a dreadful thing happened. Livingstone's station at Mabotsa, two hundred miles northeast of Moffat's station at Kuruman, was infested with lions which did a great deal of damage. Nine sheep were killed in one day, and Livingstone started out with the natives to put an end to the lions.

But instead of Livingstone killing a lion, a lion nearly killed him. Springing on him unawares from the bush, it caught him by the shoulder and shook him as a terrier dog shakes a rat. His life was saved by a kind of miracle, but the bones of his arm were crunched and broken, and the flesh torn in a terrible manner.

In this pitiable condition his thoughts turned to Kuruman as affording the best haven of rest near at hand. No place in Africa could seem so much like a home to him. For three years, while the Moffats were absent in England, it had been his headquarters, and now the Moffats were back. He had ridden a hundred and fifty miles on horseback to meet them on their way up from the Cape a few months before. So to Kuruman he went to rest and recuperate.

Notwithstanding the pain, he found himself greatly enjoying his visit. Doctor and Mrs. Moffat were both very kind to him. Mary and Ann, their charming young daughters, whose education, begun at the Cape and completed in England, soon led him to feel that there were, after all, young ladies in Africa "worth taking off his hat to"!

Before long his prejudice against the daughters of missionaries vanished away, and likewise the last remnants of his long-cherished objections to marriage disappeared. Finding in Mary, the elder, his ideal of a wife, he (to use his own words) "screwed up courage to put a question beneath one of the fruit trees." The answer to which being "Yes," the two were betrothed.

Livingstone had found his heart at last. Yet he had not obeyed its dictates without due deliberation. He had so long regarded a wife as a hindrance that he dared not "put the question beneath the fruit tree" without carefully considering what effect it might have on his future career as a missionary. This he made plain in a letter to the directors announcing that he had at last decided to marry.

Without doubt his choice was a wise one. Had he searched the world over he could not have found a more suitable bride than the one God had prepared for him in Africa. Born and bred in the country, adept in all the arts of the household, and already at work in the mission, she had every qualification for the wife of a pioneer missionary such as Livingstone then expected. At the same time, she had the culture and refinement that made her an acceptable companion for a man of such scholarly bent.

Livingstone was jubilant over the prize he had won, and became the most ardent of lovers. His betrothed was not blessed with very much of what the world would call beauty—"a little, thick, black-haired girl, sturdy, and all I want," was his description of her. Yet she had a true beauty that he was not slow to appreciate. "I see no face now to be compared with that sun-burnt one which has so often greeted me with its kind looks," he wrote her long after.

Their courtship was short, but exceedingly happy. Livingstone was fond of his jokes, and Mary Moffat knew how to take them. Notwithstanding their deep piety they were very merry together, and even in later life, when David was so famous, and both were, to all appearances, so decorous and sober, they continued to be playful at home.

The happy days at Kuruman soon came to an end. Toward the close of July Livingstone returned to Mabotsa to build a house and lay out a garden in anticipation of the coming of his bride.

At Motito, eighteen miles up from Kuruman, he wrote, on August 1, 1844, the first of his many love letters to her. In it he talks much of their plans for the future, and asks if her father will write to Colesberg about the license for their marriage. "If he cannot get it we will license ourselves," he jokingly says. Then he closes as follows:

> And now, my dearest, farewell. May God bless you! Let your affection be much more toward Him than toward me; and, kept by His mighty power and grace, I hope I shall never give you cause to regret that you have given me a part. Whatever friendship we feel toward each other, let us always look to Jesus as our common Friend and Guide, and may He shield you with His everlasting arms from every evil!

At Mabotsa, though his arm still gave him much trouble, he began at once on the house. He had almost no help, and it proved a slow and laborious task. But love spurred him on. In a letter giving an account of his progress, he wrote: "It is pretty hard work, and almost enough to drive love out of my head, but it is not situated there; it is in my heart, and won't come out unless you behave so as to quench it!"

Mary Moffat treasured the letters he wrote during their courtship as long as she lived. Years after, when they were far apart and feeling the separation most keenly, he wrote her as follows:

> You may read the letters over again that I wrote at Mabotsa, the sweet time you know. As I told you before, I tell you again, they are true, true; there is not a bit of hypocrisy in them. I never show all my feelings; but I can say truly, my dearest, that I loved you when I married you, and the longer I lived with you, I loved you the better.

Before the year closed the wedding took place, and she who bore the honored name of Moffat exchanged it for one, little known at the time, but soon to be famous throughout the whole earth.

It was a joyous and happy occasion, with few tears and no anguish at parting. The Livingstones, back in the old home in Scotland, rejoiced that their son had found such a wife, and the Moffats thanked God that their firstborn was marrying such a promising young pioneer. They would miss the dear daughter, in both the home and the mission, but she was not going very far from them and would still be in the same work as they.

The young couple proceeded at once to Mabosta. Strange to say, the name means "marriage-feast." The house was ready and the garden in beautiful order, and Mary Livingstone took up her new tasks with great ardor.

To her husband it was all joy, having her with him. "I often think of you," he wrote to his mother, "and perhaps more frequently since I got married than before. Only yesterday I said to my wife, when I thought of the nice clean bed I enjoy now, 'You put me in mind of my mother; she was always particular about our beds and our linen.' I had had rough times before."

Livingstone's marriage, connecting him with the Moffats, was one of the great providential things in his life. "No family on the face of the globe could have been so helpful to him in his great work," says Dr. Blaikie.

And no wife could have done more than his own Mary Moffat. When God called him to open up Africa, after their marriage, she could not make the long journeys with him on account of their children. She tried it at first and proved a great traveler. "Your mamma was famous for roughing it in the bush, and was never a trouble," Livingstone wrote to their daughter, after the death of her mother.

But the children suffered so much that at last she consented to take them to England and let her dear David plunge into the forest alone. It was hard, yet she had no thought of holding him back. The interests of the great continent was as dear to her as to him. Thus, for years at a time, she endured suffering, suspense, and separation, so that he might be free for the work.

Opening up Africa cost them both sore, but many shall rise up and call them blessed because of it.

JAMES GILMOUR
Emily Prankard

A Courtship by Correspondence

James Gilmour's courtship was as out-of-the-ordinary as everything else about him. Yet, like all that he did, it bore the stamp of complete consecration to God.

When he sailed for China in 1870, a strong, manly young fellow of twenty-seven, he went without either a wife or a colleague. Yet it was a lonely task that awaited him—the reopening of the London Missionary Society's long suspended work in Mongolia—and at times he was almost overwhelmed at the prospect. Before sailing he wrote:

> Companions I can scarcely hope to meet, and the feeling of being alone comes over me till I think of Christ and His blessed promise, "Lo, I

am with you always, even unto the end of the world." No one who does not go away, leaving all and being alone, can feel the force of this promise. When I begin to feel my heart threatening to go down, I betake myself to this companionship, and, thank God, I have felt the blessedness of this promise rushing over me repeatedly when I knelt down and spoke to Jesus as a present companion, from whom I am sure to find sympathy. I have felt a tingle of delight thrilling over me as I felt His presence, and thought that wherever I may go He is still with me.

On the barren plains of Mongolia, the loneliness proved ever greater than he had anticipated. Christ was indeed an ever-present friend, but young Gilmour, though so intensely in earnest, was merry and full of fun, and craved human companionship. In August, 1870, when he began his first great journey among the Mongols, a strong feeling of aversion came over him to traveling alone in a region entirely unknown to him. An unexpected companion, in the person of a Russian merchant, relieved this somewhat, but at Kiachta, the southern frontier of Siberia, the loneliness became well-nigh unbearable. During a brief period of enforced inactivity, he wrote in his diary:

Today I felt a good deal like Elijah in the wilderness. He prayed that he might die. I wonder

if I am telling the truth when I say that I felt drawn towards suicide. I take this opportunity of declaring strongly that on all occasions two missionaries should go together. I was not of this opinion a few weeks ago, but I had no idea how weak an individual I am. My eyes have filled with tears frequently these last few days in spite of myself. Oh! The intense loneliness of Christ's life, not a single one understood Him! He bore it. O Jesus, let me follow in thy steps!

At Peking, his headquarters between trips, he had no home of his own, but lived in rented rooms with a native Chinese hired servant. His meals he took with a fellow missionary, Mr. Edkins. Going to his home broke the monotony and helped not a little; nevertheless he was lonely and his life sorely lacking in comfort. His two great needs were a wife and a colleague.

The colleague he asked the directors in London to send him, whereas the wife he attempted to find for himself. A true son of Scotia, he proposed first to a Scotch girl—whether in person before he left home, or by letter from China, he has not divulged. But the Scotch girl said "No." He had asked her too late. She was already pledged to another.

His own efforts to find a wife being thus thwarted, Gilmour turned to the Lord. "I then put myself," he says, "and the direction of this affair—I mean the finding of a wife—into God's hands, asking Him to look me out one, a good one, too."

And God did what he asked.

In May, 1873, when Mr. Edkins returned to England, Gilmour lost his boarding-place. But he soon found another. Mr. Meech, an old college chum who had recently come to Peking with his bride, took him in.

In the old home in England, Mrs. Meech (née Miss Prankard, of London) had a young sister, Emily, who was inexpressibly dear to her. Coming in to his meals, Gilmour saw her picture, read extracts from her letters, and heard her praises sounded continuously. By and by he found himself so greatly attracted to the absent young lady that he wondered what it all meant. Could she be the bride God was going to give him?

Toward the close of the year, he told Mrs. Meech all about it and asked if he might correspond with her sister. She was delighted and gladly gave her consent. The prospect of having Emily with her in China filled her with joy, and she and her husband had already learned to love and trust Gilmour.

Gilmour was not slow to make use of the permission Mrs. Meech gave him. Early in January, 1874, he wrote to Miss Prankard, opening up a correspondence with her. Gilmour-like, the very first letter contained a proposal of marriage!

By the same mail he wrote to his parents in Scotland:

> I have written and proposed to a girl in England. It is true I have never seen her, and I know very little about her; but what I do know is good. Her mother supports herself and daughter by keeping a school. One of the hindrances will be perhaps that the mother will not be willing to part with her daughter, as she is, no doubt, the life of the school. I don't know, so I have written and made the offer, and leave them to decide. If she cannot come, then there is no harm done. If she can arrange to come, then my hope is fulfilled. If the young lady says "Yes," she or her friends will no doubt write you, as I have asked them to do. You may think I am rash in writing to a girl I have never seen. If you say so, I may just say that I have something of the same feeling; but what

am I to do? In addition I am very easy minded over it all, because I have exercised the best of my thoughts on the subject, and put the whole matter into the hands of God, asking Him, if it be best, to bring her, if it be not best, to keep her away, and He can manage the whole thing well.

Having posted these letters, Gilmour started on a long tour through Mongolia and tried to forget all about it.

When Emily Prankard received his letter in London, she at once took the matter to God. She had never seen this would-be husband, but she had heard much about him from her sister in China and from his friends in the homeland. The spirit of missions was strong in her heart, and at length she wrote him that she would come to China and join him in his work for Mongolia.

Receiving one another on trust from the Lord, neither of the young people took long to decide. "The first letter I wrote her was to propose," says Gilmour, "and the first letter she wrote me was to accept—romantic enough!"

Owing to a delay in the mails, the announcement did not come to the old folks in Scotland through their son's letter as he had planned, but in a note from Miss Prankard's mother in London. "My parents were scared one day last year," Gilmour wrote after his marriage, "by receiving a letter from a lady in England, a lady whose name they had not even known before, stating that her daughter had decided to become my wife! Didn't it stir up the old people! My letter to them, posted at the same time, had been delayed in London."

It was a shock at first, but Gilmour's parents soon became reconciled to his engagement. Before sailing for China, Emily Prankard spent two weeks with them in Scotland, and so completely won their hearts that they wrote to their son that "though he had searched the country for a couple of years he could not have made a better choice."

Meanwhile Gilmour himself was quietly pursuing his work on the plains of Mongolia. On the way back in July, he thought much about the question he had asked six months before. Would there be an answer waiting for him? If so, what would it be? At Kalgan he found a package of letters. One bore the London postmark and the handwriting he had grown familiar with on Mrs. Meech's letters. It was from Emily Prankard, and her answer was "Yes!"

"I proposed in January," he says, "went up to Mongolia in the spring, rode about on my camels till July, and came down to Kalgan to find that I was an accepted man!"

A short but happy courtship by correspondence followed. To his mother in Scotland he wrote:

> You will be glad to hear that I have had some delightful letters from Miss Prankard. She has written me in the most unrestrained way concerning her spiritual hopes and condition, and though we have never seen each other, yet we know more of each other's inmost life and soul than, I am quite certain, most lovers know of each other even after long personal courtship. It is quite delightful to think that even now we can talk by letter with perfect unreserve, and I tell you this because I know you will be glad to hear of it. I knew she was a pious girl, else I would not have asked her to come out to be a missionary's wife, but she turns out better even than I thought, and I am not much afraid as to how we shall get on together.

Early in the autumn, Emily Prankard sailed for China, and in November, Gilmour and Mr. Meech went to Tien-tsin to meet her. For two weeks nothing was heard of the steamer, but at length, on Sabbath evening, November 29, word came that she was outside the bar, waiting for the tide to bring her up to the city. Next morning, at five o'clock, Gilmour and Meech boarded a steam launch and started down the river. About eight o'clock they met the steamer coming up, and Mr. Meech recognized Miss Prankard on deck. But the steamer did not stop, and poor Gilmour had to wait another three hours!

Emily Prankard's first view of her beloved must have been something of a shock. "The morning was cold," says Mr. Meech, "and Gilmour was clad in an old overcoat which had seen much service in Siberia and had a woolen comforter round his neck, having more regard to warmth than appearance. We had to follow back to Tien-tsin, Gilmour being thought by those on board the steamer to be the engineer!"

But there was a charm about Gilmour that was irresistible, and, notwithstanding his unbecoming attire, Emily Prankard soon found him all she had hoped for. No one ever came within the sphere of his influence without learning to love him, and, divested of old coat and woolen comforter, he was a fine looking young fellow whom any girl might be proud to own as her lover. "There was an aspect of good humor about his face and a glance of his eye revealing any amount of fun and frolic," says one of his fellow-students. "Honesty, good nature, and true manliness were so stamped upon every feature and line of it, that you had only to see him to feel that he was one of God's noblest works, and to be drawn to him as by a magnetic influence."

On Tuesday, December 1, Miss Prankard left for Peking, escorted by Meech and Gilmour. On Thursday she reached the home of her sister, and on the following Tuesday the wedding took place. "I think I must have said 'I will' in a feeble voice," says Gilmour, "for my wife when her turn came sang out 'I will' in a voice that startled herself and me, and made it obvious how much will she was going to have in the matter!"

In a letter to his friend, Mr. Lovett, the bridegroom announced the wedding in true Gilmour-fashion as follows:

> I was married last week, Tuesday, December 8! Mrs. Meech's sister is now Mrs. Gilmour. We never saw each other until a week before we were married, and my friends here drew long faces and howled at me for being rash. What if you don't like each other? How then? It is for life! As if I didn't know all this long ago!

After a honeymoon of one week, Gilmour started out with Mr. Meech on a nine day tour into the country. Two days before Christmas he returned and settled down in Peking for a while to get acquainted with his wife. She proved all he hoped for and more. To a Scotch friend, whose letter, warning him not to take an English girl for a wife, came after his marriage, he wrote:

About my wife: as I want you to know her, I introduce you to her. She is a jolly girl, as much, perhaps more, of a Christian and a Christian missionary than I am…. The whole thing was gone about on the faith principle, and from its success, I am inclined to think more and more highly of the plan. Without any gammon, I am much happier than even in my day dreams I ever imagined I might be. It is not only me that my wife pleases, but she has gained golden opinions from most of the people who have met her among my friends and acquaintances in Scotland and China. You need not be the least bit shy of me or my English wife. She is a good lassie, any quantity better than me, and just as handy as a Scotch lass would have been. It was great fun for her to read your tirade about English wives and your warning about her. She is a jolly kind of person, and does not take offense, but I guess if she comes across you, she will shake you up a bit!

Unusual as their courtship had been, their marriage proved one of the happiest on record. In the bride God gave him, Gilmour found not only a wife, but a colleague—the only one he was ever permitted to have. Hand in hand they worked for the Mongols, her zeal fully equal to his. Delicately nurtured though she had been, this refined English lady accompanied her husband on many a long, hard journey through Mongolia, not only to relieve his loneliness, but to do her share in winning the Mongols to Christ.

For eleven years she endured privations and faced dangers of no common sort with a heroism that has rarely been equaled. Then God took her home and Gilmour was left with his motherless lads.

But she had been a great help to him, and their union the one great joy of his twenty years' lonely and difficult toil.

François Coillard & Christina Mackintosh

The Call of God in an Offer of Marriage

When François Coillard reached Leribe, Africa, in 1859, clean-shaven and unmarried, the Basutos were greatly perplexed. Could this beardless, wifeless youth be the missionary they were expecting? He was nothing but a boy!

"What could he teach?" asked the women drawing water from a little well at the close of his first day among them. "He is a young man; he has neither a wife nor a beard."

But his case was not hopeless. There were remedies for defects such as these. Coillard heard what was said, and in a very short time had grown a beard which raised him immeasurably in the eyes of the native people. He thus quickly and easily acquired one of the marks of a man among the Basutos. Would he ever acquire the other? This was a question the young Frenchman was ever asking himself.

Coillard was not without a wife because he did not want one. When the Paris Missionary Society assigned him to a lonely pioneer post, he knew he would need a woman's care and companionship. But his reverence for womanhood was so great and his ideas of matrimony were so high and exalted that he was unwilling to marry merely for the sake of comfort and companionship. He wanted a "wife from the Lord" and was willing to wait until the Lord sent her.

One evening, not long before he sailed in 1857, he thought he had found her. He had gone, as he frequently did, to the home of the rich and pious Madame André-Walther, then the rendezvous of all Protestants of note in Paris. In her brilliantly lighted salon, crowded with students and professors, deaconesses and court ladies, he was presented to a newcomer among them. Miss Christina Mackintosh by name, who had come over from Scotland to assist her sister, Miss Kate, who had been teaching for two years in Paris.

From the moment they met, Coillard knew that Christina Mackintosh was the wife he wanted. But

he said nothing to her. There was no time for their acquaintance to ripen into even an ordinary friendship, and he feared to act on such a sudden impulse lest it be a mere human desire and not "of the Lord." So he sailed away without revealing the hope in his heart that someday she would come to Africa and share his work for the Basutos.

The foundations of his hope were very slight. There was no ground for it whatever save that he knew her heart was in the mission field. When little more than a child, she had resolved to be a missionary to Africa. But this purpose had lain dormant until an address of his own, which she had heard soon after coming to Paris, revived it again.

Nevertheless the vision went with him. Throughout the long journey by sea and by land the conviction steadily grew that she was "The One."

At length, in obedience to what he believed to be divine guidance, he wrote from Africa, offering her his heart and his hand. In the orthodox fashion of France, the proposal was made through their mutual friend, Madame Walther.

Six months passed and then came her answer—a refusal on the ground that she did not know him well enough! This was true. Yet had it not been for the storm of opposition it raised, her answer might have been different. She had heard God calling her to Africa, and she had seen enough of Coillard to know that he was one of the noblest and most lovable of men.

Her sister Kate alone favored her going. She had known Coillard in Paris, and felt that it was an honor for her sister to be asked to share the life of this heroic young missionary. But everyone else was opposed to it. Her mother refused to entertain the idea. Even Coillard's friends, as well as her own, expressed their disapproval very frankly. She was implored not to bury her talents in Africa, and he was warned that a young woman who was more at home in the classroom than the kitchen would be a hindrance instead of a help. So Christina, strong and self-reliant though she was, yielded to the opposition and stayed at home.

But from now on she devoted every spare moment to work among the poor—to quiet her conscience, perhaps.

It was a sore disappointment to Coillard, and a great test of his faith. He had been so sure she would come. But it was all a part of God's plan. At this time Coillard was somewhat lacking in self-confidence, and much too dependent on human sympathy and help. But now, alone with the heathen, he learned to find God all in all. It was a sore experience, but it gave him new beauty and strength.

But it was hard. Entries in his diary and letters to his mother show how intensely he suffered from isolation among a people entirely heathen. The loneliness was almost unbearable, and added to it were the burdens of housekeeping, with no help save from careless and incompetent natives, who spoiled his food and smashed his dishes.

For two years Coillard worked on alone, one of the world's real heroes. He put away all thought of marriage, yet ever and anon there came to him the vision of a face with sparkling eyes—not beautiful, perhaps, but calm and restful and full of resolute purpose. He could not banish it, do what he would, and it filled him with longing. It was the face of Christina, the girl who would not come.

Did she ever think of him, alone in Africa, and suffering so? Had she ever regretted the answer she gave? Would it be any use to ask her again? He needed her so much, and so did the work! What could he not do with her to help him! At length, having sought counsel of God, he wrote again, and this time the answer was different.

Christina now perceived that it was God who was calling her—that this twice-repeated offer of marriage was her opportunity for fulfilling her early vow to be a missionary. Viewed in this light, she dared not decline it. So she wrote she would come.

There was opposition still, but not from those nearest and dearest. God had been working in her mother's heart, and she was now able to make the sacrifice with joy. "I would rather see my daughter a missionary than a princess," she wrote to her soon-to-be son-in-law.

Coillard's cup overflowed when he received Christina's acceptance. "I cannot believe in my own happiness," he wrote in his diary on July 5, 1860, the day her answer arrived. It had a good effect, too, on his work. "Molapo, now that he knows I am going to be married, acquaints me with all his affairs, and demands my advice," he wrote of the chief a month later.

Knowing how much she was needed, Christina resolved to sail for Africa before the end of the year. On July 5, the very day her letter reached Leribe, she left Paris and started for Scotland to prepare for the wedding. "It was a terrible wrench to leave everything dear to her," says her niece. "She had no illusions as to what kind of a life awaited her, and it was not the kind she liked. She preferred civilization to the wilds."

Coillard knew something of what it was costing and was full of tenderest sympathy for her. "I do not know that I could do what you are doing," he wrote her, "giving up all for an unknown country and an almost unknown husband."

The knowledge that it was God's will alone sustained her. This also Coillard knew and appreciated. "How happy I am," he wrote later, "to see that you perceive clearly the will of God in our union. Later on that will be a source of strength and comfort. For in the days of disappointment and trial, when Satan will whisper, 'What are you doing here?', you will be able to answer, 'God, my God, bade me go, and I have obeyed.' May I, by my constant love, fill all the empty places in your heart."

Of her letters to him at this time only one has survived. One passage in it shows how eagerly she welcomed anything that added to the tie between them. "What do you say, dear Frank, to this letter all in English?" she wrote. "It would have been sad for me to write you in a foreign language from home, for I cling so to your having this at least in common to those dear to me, that you understand their tongue as well as your own."

In the autumn Christina went to Asnieres in France to make the acquaintance of Coillard's mother, to whom he was devotedly attached. During this visit, which ever remained a precious memory to both, Madame Coillard gave her a packet of François' letters to read—letters which revealed the depths of love and tenderness in his nature, and showed how much he had suffered without her in Africa. These, more than anything else, braced her for the coming ordeal of breaking home ties. "What gave you such a happy thought?" Coillard wrote to his mother. "Not that my letters are worth much, but because they could cheer my betrothed amid all the sorrows of parting, by assuring her that an affectionate son would not be an unloving husband."

On November 23, 1860, Christina sailed for Africa on the *John Williams*. "Such grief I never saw, and can hardly bear to think of now," her sister wrote forty-five years after. But the peace of God soon filled her heart.

Meanwhile, in Africa, Coillard's people were awaiting her coming with a joy scarcely less than his own. "Today you are a man," they said, when he started to the Cape to meet her. "Return quickly and bring us our mother and the mother of our wives!"

Through a misunderstanding, due to a mix-up in the mails, Coillard went to Port Elizabeth, whereas Christina landed at Cape Town. Without waiting for a boat to take him around by the sea, he started in hot haste across country. There was some danger involved, but he cared nothing for this. It saved so much time! But when the news of his breakneck journey reached Paris, the Director sent him an official rebuke "for risking his life to save a few days' time in what was not strictly the business of his calling"—a rebuke tempered, however, by an unofficial postscript saying that he was "happy all the same to have such proof that chivalry was not yet dead among the sons of France!"

Christina's first words to her lover were the heroic ones that formed the keynote of all her legacy. "I have come," she said, "to do the work of God with you, whatever it may be; and remember this: wherever God may call you, you shall never find me crossing your path of duty."

The wedding took place on February 26, 1861, in the Union Church at Cape Town. Immediately thereafter, Monsieur and Madame Coillard began their long wedding journey to their distant field. It was accomplished in the regulation, slow-going, South African ox wagon, but Christina, knowing her husband's intense love of the beautiful, had bent all her energies toward making it pretty and homelike. He was delighted, and wrote to her sister, "Everyone is astounded in admiring the taste that has decorated it. People can't believe it is a traveling wagon, it is so fresh and mignon, with its pretty curtains, its elegant pockets hung on either side, the leopard skin, the plants, etc., the whole forming, one would think, the eighth wonder of the world."

Christina was very happy all the way up from the Cape. The devotion of her husband, the beauty of the scenery, and the warm welcome of the missionaries through whose stations they passed, made the journey a joy. But after a few weeks at Leribe, homesickness and the change in climate combined to make her ill, and she grew listless and weary. During the day she bravely kept at her work, but in the evenings she sat pouring over old letters and journals that made the tears flow very fast. But one day, when alone in the house, she suddenly realized that this was all wrong, and, gathering up the precious memorials of the past, she threw them into the fire! When her husband returned, she met him at the door, saying, "I have burned them all. You shall never see me fretting again. Forget thine own people and thy father's house!"

Thenceforth, says her niece, "their life was an unbroken idyll of thirty years." She continues:

> Of their mutual happiness it seems almost sacrilege to write, yet something must be said of a union so perfect begun in circumstances so unusual. Knowing that it was not self-will, but God's Providence, that had brought them together, each accepted the other with absolute confidence, as a gift from Him, and hence as one to be cherished and held sacred for the sake of the Giver. The changes and trials of their career only served to bring out fresh perfections in each other's eyes, so that their whole married life was one long series of delightful surprises, a never-ending romance.

To their sore disappointment God gave them no children. But the withholding of this served only to draw them closer together, and to enable them to give themselves wholly to Africa.

For thirty years they worked hand in hand, he a hero and she a heroine of no common sort. When he went on long exploring tours into the wilderness, his wife went with him doing her share of the work and supplying the neatness, the cleanliness, and the touches of beauty that meant so much to one of his high-strung, sensitive nature.

In God's arithmetic one and one make more than two. "One man shall chase a thousand, and two shall put ten thousand to flight." Never was this truer than in the case of the Coillards. Either alone would have made a great missionary. Together they accomplished a work for Africa that was great beyond measure.

HENRY MARTYN & Lydia Grenfell

The Handicap of a Hopeless Attachment

To marry or not to marry—this was Henry Martyn's question—whether it were better to serve God by remaining single or by taking to himself a wife.

He was only nineteen, this brilliant young student who had found Christ at Cambridge, and was giving up all to God. For Christ's sake he had already sacrificed his chosen profession, the law, and now came this question of marriage. Back in Cornwall, not far from the old home in Truro, there was a young lady, Lydia Grenfell by name, whom he greatly admired. He hoped to woo her some day and make her his wife. Must this be added to his other sacrifices?

Ere long the question seemed answered. Charles Simeon won him for missions, and he resolved to go out under the Church Missionary Society at his own charges. But his income was not sufficient for two. So he put away all thoughts of marriage.

Yet the question was far from being settled. By and by his friends began to feel that such a saintly young scholar could do more for God as a chaplain of the East India Company than as a missionary. It would give him great prestige and open wide doors of opportunity in India. But Martyn shrank from its subtle temptations. The salary was large, and a wife almost a necessity, and he was grieved to find dreams of marriage again creeping into his heart.

Early in 1804, an event occurred which made it necessary for him to go as a chaplain or not at all. He and his sisters lost all their patrimony through a disaster in Cornwall. The younger, being unmarried, was left without means of support, and Martyn felt that he ought to assume it. But the salary of a missionary was not sufficient for this. So, on the advice of his friends, he applied for a chaplaincy. Being promised the next vacant post, he went down to Cornwall in June to spend his vacation and take leave of his loved ones. Both parents were dead, but his sisters were there, and Miss Grenfell.

Bittersweet were the days that he spent there. Lydia proved more charming than ever, but

marriage was out of the question. Even a chaplain's salary, large as it was, would not support both a wife and a sister.

Miss Grenfell's home at Marazion was only twenty-six miles from Truro, yet for over a week Martyn made no attempt to see her. On the last Sunday in June, when he went to St. Hilary (not far from Marazion) to preach in Cornwall's famous old church, he hoped to find her in the congregation. But she did not come and he suffered the keenest disappointment. Yet, in his pain, he thanked God for keeping her away, as she might have proved a distraction.

In the evening after tea he went to call on her, and that night gave her large space in that famous journal in which henceforth her name appears on almost every page.

"Called after tea on Miss L. G.," the poor young fellow wrote, "and walked with her and —, conversing on spiritual subjects. All the rest of the evening, and at night, I could not keep her out of my mind. I felt too plainly that I loved her passionately. The direct opposition of this to my devotedness to God in the missionary way excited no small tumult in my mind. I continued an hour and a half in prayer striving against this attachment. I was about to triumph, but in a moment my heart had wandered back to the beloved idol again."

A month later, when he returned to Cambridge, the farewells cost him sore. "Parted with Lydia, perhaps forever in this life, with a sort of uncertain pain which I knew would increase to greater violence afterward," his journal says. And thus it proved. Yet cost what it might, he resolved to be true to his missionary vow. That night, ere he slept, he made a rededication of himself to God. "Never," says Miss Yonge, "were hopes and affections more thoroughly sacrificed."

Meanwhile what about Lydia? Did she return Martyn's affection? Apparently not at this time. She had known him for years (her sister Emma had married his cousin) and she admired him greatly. But she was six years his senior, and her mind was too much taken up with a former love affair to think much about him. The young man to whom she had been engaged proved unworthy, and afterwards married another; yet she had an idea that her promise to him was binding as long as he lived.

Her sister, however, thought she cared more for Martyn than she was willing to show, and told him so when he confided in her the story of his love on the way back to London. This gave him pain as well as pleasure, and added to the intensity of his affection.

Nevertheless he adhered to his resolution not to marry. But before leaving England, the question came up again for discussion. At a meeting of the Eclectic Society of which he was a member, one of his friends told him that he "was acting like a madman to go out unmarried." All the other ministers present expressed the same views, and poor Martyn was sorely perplexed. His sister having been recently betrothed to a worthy young man, he was now free to marry. Was this God's way of revealing His will?

"When I think of Brainerd," he wrote at this time, "how he lived among the Indians, traveling freely from place to place, can I conceive that he would have been so useful had he been married? Schwartz was never married, nor was Paul. On the other hand, I have often thought how valuable would be the counsel and comfort of a Christian brother in India. These advantages would be obtained by marrying. I am utterly at a loss to know what is best."

His friends would not let the matter drop, and at length he wrote to Mr. Simeon. While awaiting his answer the Tempter stood by. "I have not felt such pain since I parted from Lydia in Cornwall," he says. "I could not help saying, 'Go, Hindus, go on in your misery; let Satan still rule over you; he who is appointed to labor over you is consulting his ease.' No, thought I, hell and earth shall never keep me back from my work." When Simeon's letter came, it contained such weighty arguments against his marrying that he acquiesced at once.

On July 17, 1805, the young chaplain sailed from Portsmouth on the *Union*, one of a large fleet bound for the East. As he slowly sailed past the coasts of Devonshire and his beloved Cornwall, the thought of the loved ones there well-nigh broke his heart. He thought he had parted from them forever, but he was soon to see them again. On the 19th, to his great surprise, the fleet anchored off Falmouth, not far from his home! While awaiting orders from Nelson it remained there three weeks.

At first Martyn made no attempt to see Lydia, though she was only twenty miles away. But ere long love conquered, and, having first asked God to prevent it if it be contrary to His will, he boarded the coach for Marazion, and, with much confusion, told her of his love, and asked if she would come out to him if it seemed best for him to marry in India. But she would not commit herself, and he returned to Falmouth greatly depressed.

On August 10 he went to pay her what proved his last visit. At five that morning a signal had sounded announcing the sailing of the fleet. But he did not know it until about nine, when, as he sat reading the Scriptures to Lydia and her mother, a messenger arrived saying that a friend was waiting at St. Hilary with a carriage to take him to Falmouth.

"It came upon me like a thunderbolt," says the poor young lover. "Lydia was evidently painfully affected by it; she came out with me that we might be alone at taking leave, and I then told her that she must not be offended at receiving a letter from me from India. In the great hurry she discovered more of her mind than she intended; she made no objection whatever to coming out. Thinking perhaps I wished to make an engagement with her, she said we had better go quite free. With this I left her."

By dint of hard riding Martyn reached Falmouth in time. But he had a narrow escape. The fleet was well underway, but the *Union*, having become entangled in the chains, had been unable to clear the harbor. The captain was vexed, but Martyn thanked God, and Lydia wrote in her diary: "Doth not God care for His own, and order everything that concerns them? The fleet must not sail till the man of God joined it; praised be the name of the Lord."

Lydia's sorrow, though not so keen, was now akin to Martyn's own. It sometimes happens that love begets love, and it had evidently been so in her case. "Much have I to testify of supporting grace this day," she wrote in her diary on August 10, after their final parting. "My affections are engaged past recalling, and the anguish I endured yesterday, from an apprehension that I had treated him with coolness, exceeds my power to express; but God saw it, and kindly ordered that he should come and do away the idea from my mind. It contributed likewise to my peace, and I hope to his, that it is clearly now understood between us that he is free to marry where he is going, and I have felt quite resigned to the will of God in this, and shall often pray the Lord to find him a suitable partner." Little did she know her own heart!

Two months after landing at Calcutta, Martyn received a packet of letters from home. There was one from Lydia and one from Charles Simeon sounding her praises. Having recently made her acquaintance, he now expressed regret that she had not gone to India with Martyn. Poor Martyn! Did ever a man suffer more at the hands of his friends?

The next day he told his brother chaplain, David Brown, all about it. Mr. Brown assured him that a wife would be a great help in the work, and advised him to send for Lydia. So, on July 30, 1806, after many days of deliberation and prayer, he wrote her a long and loving letter asking if she would come.

At Dinapore, whither he was sent in October, he waited long for an answer. The heat was excessive, the work heavy, and his strength beginning to fail. Yet he labored incessantly and gave much time to prayer.

He greatly needed a wife. He had plenty of servants, but no one to watch over him and make him take care of himself. His salary was ample, but his great house with its spacious rooms and wide verandas was entirely lacking in comforts. Mrs. Sherwood, who with her husband was Martyn's guest for two days, tells how much she suffered for want of a pillow. Her face ached badly at night, but she could find nothing to lay her head on but "a bolster stuffed as hard as a pin-cushion!"

But she found much to admire in Martyn him-self. In her autobiography she gives a charming picture of him as she knew him in his Indian home. "He was dressed in white and looked very pale," she says, "which, however, was nothing singular in India. His hair, a light brown, was raised from his forehead, which was a remarkably fine one. His features were not regular, but the expression was so luminous, so intellectual, so affectionate, so beaming with divine charity, that no one could have looked at his features and thought of their form. He was as remarkable for ease as for cheerfulness, and had a rich, deep voice and fine taste for music. When he relaxed from his labors in the presence of his friends, it was to laugh and play like a happy, innocent child, especially if there were children to laugh and play with him."

It was weary waiting for Lydia. "Ever, through the solitude, the suffering, and the toiling of the first twelve months at Dinapore," says Dr. George Smith, "the thought of Lydia Grenfell, the hope of her union to him, and her help in his agonizing for India, runs like a chord of sad music." Once he dreamed she had come, but awoke with a sigh to find it only a dream. "Perhaps all my hope about her is but a dream!" he wrote the next day in his diary. "Yet be it so; whatever God shall appoint must be good for us both, and I will endeavor to be tranquil and happy, pursuing my way through the wilderness with equal steadiness, whether with or without a companion."

At last, on October 24, 1807, after more than a year of suspense, her answer reached Dinapore—a refusal on the ground that her mother would not give her consent.

It was a blow that well-nigh crushed Martyn. "Lydia refuses to come because her mother will not give her consent," he wrote to the Rev. David Brown, who had advised him to send for her. He continued:

> Sir, you must not wonder at my pale looks when I receive so many hard blows on my heart. Yet a Father's love appoints the trial, and I pray that it may have its intended effect. Yet, if you wish to prolong my existence in this world, make a representation to some persons at home who may influence her friends. Your word will be believed sooner than mine. The extraordinary effect of mental disorder on my bodily frame is unfortunate; trouble brings on disease and disorders the sleep. In this way I am laboring a little now, but not much; in a few days it will pass away again. He that hath delivered and doth deliver, is He in whom we trust that He will yet deliver.... The queensware on its way to me can be sold at an outcry or sent to Corrie. I do not want queensware or anything else now. My new house and garden, without the person I expected to share it with me, excite disgust.

On the receipt of Lydia's letter, Martyn wrote at once to ask whether, if he agreed not to urge her to leave her mother, she would consent to an engagement in order that they might still correspond. But she refused this too, and bade him a final farewell.

It broke Martyn's heart and cost her much sorrow. Why, then, did she not go? To Charles Simeon, who went to intercede for his beloved young friend, she gave four reasons—her health, the indelicacy of going out to India alone on such an errand, her former engagement to another man, and the unwillingness of her mother to give her consent.

But these—alas!—were excuses, rather than insurmountable obstacles. Had she really wanted to go, the first three would have carried no weight, and the fourth would doubtless have yielded to prayer and persuasion. Her diary is full of intense love and devotion to God, but one may search its pages in vain for a single sentence expressing a desire to join her suitor in India and share in his work. She loved Martyn and she loved God, but not enough to make such a sacrifice. The poet probed deep into her heart and laid bare its secrets when he wrote:

> *The woman of his love*
> *Feared to leave all and give her life to his,*
> *And both to God.*

Yet few dare blame her. Let those heroic souls whose sacrifices match those of a Christina Coillard or an Ann Judson cast the first stone.

Thus ended Henry Martyn's wooing. But his friends were loath to let the matter drop. They thought he needed a wife and when the sister of his dear friend, the Rev. Daniel Corrie, came to join her brother in India it was suggested that perhaps she might be the one. By and by a rumor reached England that they were soon to be married. Lydia heard it and was greatly disturbed! Simeon heard it and wrote to David Brown to confirm it.

"How could you imagine" Brown wrote back, "that Miss C. would do as well as Miss L. G. for Mr. Martyn? Dear Martyn is married already to three wives, whom I believe he would not forsake for all the princesses on earth—I mean his three translations of the Holy Scriptures."

Ill health, lack of visible results, his hopeless attachment, and the death of both sisters, leaving him the last of his family, filled Martyn's cup of sorrow full to overflowing, yet he continued to work without ceasing. When the news of the death of his second sister reached him in March, 1810, his grief was excessive. But Lydia now took compassion on him and wrote offering to take the place of her who was gone. This acted as balm to his sorrowing heart. "My long lost Lydia consents to write to me," he wrote to David Brown.

The correspondence that followed was the great solace of the two weary years that remained. He had given her up but she was ever "his dearest," and the last letter he wrote was to her.

On October 16, 1812, when Martyn "burned out for God" at Tokat, he was only thirty-one. Humanly speaking, had Lydia been there, he need not have died. With a wife to care for and comfort and cheer him his life might have been lengthened and his service for India greatly prolonged. "It was the greatest calamity of his whole career that Lydia did not accompany him," says Doctor George Smith. "But we cannot consider it a 'bitter misfortune' as some do, that he ever knew her. His love for her worked a higher elevation for himself and gives to his Letters and Journals an intense human interest."

Lydia Grenfell saved herself; but she cut short and marred Martyn's career, and lost the high honor of being his wife. Would her decision be different, could she come back and live her life over?*

---

* See pages 78–82 for a critique of the author's analysis of Lydia Grenfell's decision.

ONE-OARED BOATS

an afterword by David Hosaflook

"A missionary without a wife in this country is like a boat with one oar," wrote then-single missionary Robert Moffat. He was in love with Mary Smith and was acknowledging his loneliness in the style of an African proverb.

I can relate! I was a single missionary for five years. I know the feeling of rowing alone on a faraway river, wondering if my course—ever distancing itself from my native culture and flowing into another—would ever lead to marriage. This feeling led me into some embarrassing interactions. I confess to some cringe-worthy attempts at romance, a few hasty, Gilmour-like maneuvers that did not end well. (*Caution, men. Get counsel before making fools of yourselves. Trust me on this.*) Loneliness can lead to erratic behavior, as illustrated by some of the stories in this book, and as I painfully recall from my youth. I admit all this to demonstrate my, *ahem*, "credentials" to opine a little on matters of missionary romance.

Fortunately, my story also includes a romance that *did* work out well—indeed more beautifully than I deserve. I am deeply grateful for my bride. She is a gift from the Lord who has endured much during our twenty-four years of marriage: riots, anarchy, threats, earthquakes, caring for me, and the usual heartbreaks and hardships of leaving home permanently to serve in a less developed country. We have reared six children together on the foreign field, three by adoption. They all rise up with me to bless her. I thank her for saying yes.

The topic of this book is uniquely attractive—missions and love. What a match! Several years ago I was invited to speak at a large missionary conference for students. I presented a workshop entitled "Romance on the Mission Field," not because I am a particularly successful love doctor, but because I have experienced both missionary lives, single and married, and have endured the difficult and awkward transition between the two. Later I felt bad for the other presenters of that workshop hour, because my session was jam-packed. It was difficult to compete with such a topic at such a venue!

In the preface to this book I warned you that Belle Brain's love stories raise questions about singleness, marriage, and various dynamics of missionary romance, and that I would attempt to debrief with you in this afterword. My background and experience, I hope, gives me something helpful to offer. I love talking about missions, especially with younger missionaries, so pretend we are chatting informally about the book over a cup of strong espresso at a Balkan coffee bar.

Belle has given us a true gift, a lovely bouquet of a half-dozen vignettes. The historian in me advises you to get into the primary sources—the missionaries' journals and correspondence—if you really want to understand their love lives and how they processed matters of romance. But Belle has opened a window to introduce us, at least, to the personal lives of men and women we highly regard in our church history. She allows us to see ordinariness in their greatness. I love this about missionary biographies. Despite being set in bygone centuries, we relate to the experiences they faced. In this intriguing theme of romance, it is hard not to smile when reading about emotions we have felt ourselves, struggles we have fought, even extreme measures we have taken to manage our loneliness.

As we read, we find that the author has also given us a prompt to think about all sorts of important and controversial topics related to missions and marriage: trust in God, relationships with others, the benefits and limitations of both singleness and marriage, loneliness, the struggles families face on the field, the underestimated role and trials of parents who consecrate their children to missions, depression, suicidal thoughts, plain common sense, encouragement, and many more.

Thank you, Belle!

Regretfully, however, we must also address what I think is the elephant in the room—the harsh words in the final paragraphs. I was shocked (were you?) to see Lydia Grenfell get blamed for ruining Henry Martyn's career and causing his early demise! When I first read this I exclaimed, "*Wait, what?!*" and had to re-read it to make sure I had not misunderstood.

I disagreed so strongly that I could not republish this book without responding, hoping to correct what seems like Belle's overzealous attempt to end her book with a powerful, pensive punch. Since it comes at Lydia's expense and risks promoting bad reasoning, I offer a rebuttal.

While I empathize with Belle's dismay about the dearth of volunteers and agree with her that issues of love have hindered far too many would-be missionaries, she has simply gone too far. She leaves us with the impression that if a good missionary asks a woman to marry him, she is obliged to agree, lest she be found guilty of thwarting the mission of God. That puts men in a most convenient position when seeking a young lady's hand! If she does not want to marry him and does not believe God is leading her to join him in his mission, by Belle's standards she is trapped. She must either consent against her better judgment or risk going down in infamy as someone who "saved herself." *Nonsense!*

This mindset also assumes that if a single man and woman disagree on God's plan for their futures together (or non-plan), the man's opinion should trump the woman's, especially if he is a missionary. I cannot think of any biblical support for this notion, even within the framework of the most conservative models of women's roles in the church and home.

My wife tells the story of a college boy who informed her, quite matter-of-factly, that God had told him they should be together. She calmly informed him that she happened to know God, too, but that He had not informed *her* of any such plan. *Ouch!* But good for her! It was tantamount to spiritual blackmail and she called him out on it.

It is easy, dear singles, to mistake loneliness and biology for the voice of God when you are attracted to a person. But it is harder to mistake God's voice when it comes to you through the person's clear answer of "No!" (or their deafening silence). The Holy Spirit is wise and powerful enough to change the person's affections and choices, just as He did in the case of Christina Mackintosh, but He does not need our help to accelerate that process. Single women, if your sanctified equivalent to eyelash-batting has failed to get a guy's attention, just leave it to God and keep serving Him with joy. Men, if your wooing has failed and your only recourse is to try guilting the girl into joining you, please just give up and move on.

Quickly!

Poor Lydia Grenfell! She was a godly woman who served faithfully in her church. After reading Belle's harsh final paragraph, I wanted to go back in time, meet Lydia and tell her I appreciate her commitment to Christ. We have every reason to assume the best of her and affirm her agonizing decision to reject Henry Martyn's offer. She was six years older than him, had health problems, was struggling with her own broken engagement, and, it seems, did not love Henry in the way he wanted. She apparently had no particular passion for India and no sense that God was leading her into missions. These are not indicators of a spiritual deficiency in her. She respected Martyn greatly and loved him as a brother in Christ. It appears she simply believed she would hinder his career if they married—the very thing, ironically, Brain has accused her of by her refusal.

Furthermore, Lydia's mother objected to the marriage. It is inconsistent of the author to commend Mary Smith and Robert Moffat for patiently honoring Mary's parents, then to castigate Lydia for honoring hers. Lydia Grenfell was neither the cause of, nor the solution to, Henry Martyn's struggles and health problems.

This is not to say I have no sympathy for Henry! Unrequited love is a hard pill to swallow, especially in a faraway and lonely outpost. Just as I will not criticize Lydia for saying no, I will not criticize Henry for hoping against hope for a yes. He suffered as a single and longed for the deep companionship of marriage. If it is true, however, that Lydia had become "a beloved idol" to him (as he put it), we may justifiably wonder how well *he* was handling the situation. He was indeed a great missionary—one of the greatest—but that does not mean he would have been an ideal husband and father. Many great missionaries were not (just read about the controversial marriage and parenting of William Carey, "the father of modern missions").

In Belle Brain's estimation, Lydia "lost the high honor of being Martyn's wife." She suggests Lydia would redo it all if she could. My sense is that she would not. She felt honored enough to be asked, but prioritized keeping a clear conscience before God, a conscience that was telling her she could not marry him. Henry, on the other hand, may have redone some things if he could. Perhaps he would choose to stand down and accept Lydia's entreaty to move on and find someone else. We can only speculate—but that does not mean we ought to. Let their stories be theirs and let ours be ours. We should spend more time considering how we can "redo" the day we shall have tomorrow, using it more effectively for the glory of God than we used today.

The confluence of two powerful rivers, missions and romance, makes for a turbulent ride, and each missionary must look to Scripture for guidance and seek counsel for their specific situations.

Many missionaries love Christ enough to give up the prospect of married life, but still feel a deep desire for companionship. The problem Belle Brain wanted to target through her book was the reluctance of *female* missionaries to join the growing crop of *males*. Today the opposite is true. There are more *ladies* in "one-oared boats" than *men*. In the 1800s, the idea of sending single missionary ladies was not yet mainstream. In time, as more and more missionary wives discovered ministry niches that only women could do effectively, single women began joining missionary teams. Skipping forward to our own day, statistics show that as many as 85% of single Evangelical missionaries are female. Praise God for them—but where are their brothers? Men, may we not be intimidated by the strength and example of our brave-hearted sisters, but rather inspired to action by their initiative and zeal, joining their ranks.

In 1 Corinthians 7, Paul commended unmarried ministry and gave convincing arguments for its superiority. Single missionaries can focus exclusively on "the things of the Lord," not on "worldly things," he says. They don't have to worry about things like diamonds or diapers. They have more time to learn languages and take the Gospel further down rivers and higher up mountains.

During my five "Pauline" years, I survived on little money and little sleep. I "made tents" (drove UPS trucks) to support my ministry, hiked to scores of remote mountain villages—sometimes using a literal "boat with one oar"—and achieved native-level fluency in my target language. They were momentum-building years. A church movement was planted. Shepherd boys I discipled then are now shepherding churches. I devoted all my time to worship and mission. May God be praised.

So to the single missionaries reading this book, I urge you to "seize the day." Enjoy your singularity of focus. Grow increasingly content and joyful *in Christ alone* and accomplish as much as you can while you have such a flexible schedule and exponentially efficient days.

Someday you may get married and have children, and you will discover a different kind of culture shock. It is why Paul wrote what he did. If you want a small taste of 1 Corinthians 7:33–34, visit a baby superstore. Look at the women, most of them pregnant. They are locked in and laser-focused on their God-given instinct to nurture their coming babies. Now look at the men, some becoming first-time dads. Many of them are dizzy and reeling. They are in culture shock, just beginning to perceive the cataclysmic changes coming to their world. If you get married, that will become your world, too. Marriage is a life changer even without the complexities of navigating culture stress on a foreign field. It will change your world forever, adding limitations and obligations (and *opportunities*, as I shall explain later).

I remember discussing this issue with a married missionary. He was grappling with the fact that most of the men he wanted to reach gathered in the evenings, talking to each other at the coffee bars late into the night, just when he and his family would be settling down for supper and bedtime. He was struggling to find a creative way to be both a good dad and a good evangelist. Single missionaries would have a simple solution: stay up late engaging the men and sleep in the next day.

Through Moses, God has told us that it is not good for man to be alone, but through Paul, God is telling singles to consider remaining single. This commendation implies that you have a choice in the matter, as if perfect candidates are lining up. Many of you do not have this luxury (or liability, if you prefer). You are not seeing any viable options for marriage at the moment.

One of my Bible teachers taught that the way to know you are gifted and called to be single is not a *desire* to stay single forever (which few singles have), but rather the *condition* of being single. That is, if you are single now, be assured God has equipped you with every grace not merely to *be* single—but also to *be content* as a single. Does not God promise to supply your every need? To sustain you through any temptation? This means that if you are *not* married yet, you do not *need* to be married yet, despite how much you may want it.

When I was single, I wanted to be married. I appreciated 1 Corinthians 7:33–34, but it was not enough to make me a Franciscan or make me close my eyes whenever a girl crossed my path. Rather, it became a response text or "fighter verse" when my heart lurched towards discontent and self-pity. It comforted me when an engagement fell through and when a "hopeful attachment" failed to materialize. What a blessing, I thought, to be more free to devote myself fully to the Lord's work! I had to be careful, however, not to allow Paul's passage to become a springboard to "sour grapes," cynicism, or feelings of superiority towards the married missionaries who had to care "for worldly things." (Oh, the depths of pride God exposes in His servants!)

Missionary biographies and journals helped me while I was single. How encouraging to read words like Gilmour's on the promise of the presence of Jesus in the Great Commission: "No one who does not go away, leaving all and being alone, can feel the force of this promise."

I laughed at episodes like the one described by David Livingstone about people back home who were denouncing his singleness and insinuating he was merely unable to find a spouse. It reminded me of some well-meaning Christians in my own home churches who always seemed to have a romance tip, blind date idea, or interrogation about why I was not interested in this or that girl. Ah, the beloved "peanut gallery"! Their implication was that non-married life and ministry was inferior to married life, that I was somehow less fulfilled or less effective. I had to hold my tongue to not make some snarky comment about Jesus and Paul being single. I felt uncomfortable when people interpreted my non-interest in a particular girl as a lack of appreciation for her, or when they insinuated that I was pretentious with an impossible standard. I felt validated to read about other missionaries facing these very kinds of things.

I resonated with Robert Moffat, who described being crushed with sorrow when his beloved told him her father had closed the door permanently, and how his sorrow only drew him closer to God. François Coillard described his pain when Christina Mackintosh "would not come" to Africa. Belle Brain explains it thus: "He had been so sure she would come." That phrase recalled a poem I had written in the 1990s entitled "She Will Come" (whoever *she* would be). I composed the poem on a chilly autumn night, sitting on a stone bench in the yellow light of a buzzing, flickering street lamp. Several months had passed since a Scottish girl had unexpectedly broken our engagement for reasons I failed to comprehend. I had moved on in my heart, but was still healing. I still desired a life companion.

People had told me that when they surrendered their need to be married, only then did God provide them a wife. At times, I think, I tried to use reverse psychology to convince God (and myself) that I had *truly* surrendered my need, half expecting that after my "Amen," I would open my eyes and see The One. That formula did not succeed. But on that bench, God settled my heart and gave it resolution. The bench became an altar and the moment was a turning point. I have not shared this poem with anyone until now, but maybe it will help someone:

> As leaves did turn on oak and vine
> And weather warned of aging Time,
> I said that she would come.
>
> When other doors the Lord did close,
> With sometimes woeful heart
> I chose to hope that she would come
>
> When swelling hopes had reached their ends;
> When Tear and Lonely were my friends,
> I prayed that she would come.
>
> When walking back to empty home
> While knowing I was all alone,
> I begged that she would come.
>
> As God Omniscient slowed His man,
> Revealing, some, His sacred plan,
> I doubted she would come.

In time, alone, in solitude,
I learned my heart had misconstrued
This need that she must come.

A wily plot, indeed, a lie
To think *true joy* would multiply
Somehow if she should come.

For all my joy is fully met
In knowing One who now has let
Me see that *He has come.*

The leaves are turning once again.
He knows if she will come.

The final lines tested the boundaries of my trust in God's wisdom and omniscience, leaving me feeling vulnerable, but I had learned that in Christ I was completely fulfilled. I could be satisfied in singleness while still hopeful for marriage. Neither condition brings joy and no condition should produce despair. The sufficiency of Christ enabled me to entrust all the "ifs" in my life to Him.

A supporting church sent me a powerful sermon preached by their young pastor, a friend of mine, whose wife was on her death bed. It was based on Daniel 3:16–18 (the fiery furnace) and entitled "But If Not". God is able to save us through the fires, *but if not*, we can be assured He will be with us, allowing only the ropes that bind us to burn away (Daniel 3:24–25). The pastor's wife actually passed away before I received the sermon cassette in the mail, so it was especially emotional and powerful. In a moment, this young man was single again. Our friendship grew and he began encouraging me, as did others. I discovered that God provides all the companionship we *need* as we wait for the kind of companionship we *want*.

Since I am now happily married and republishing this book, you may correctly assume that, despite all I have said in support of unmarried missionary service, I prefer marriage!

I love my *two-oared* boat (or *eight-oared*, if you count my kids). Although my one-oared boat was smaller, went faster, and required fewer pit stops, it was flimsy and lacked gravitas, direction, fellowship and certain graces. You might say that marriage transforms a man's boat into a ship.

Yes, there are advantages to singleness, but also disadvantages. Belle Brain illustrated this when she described how François Coillard's people in Basutoland took him less seriously because he had no wife and no beard. He grew the beard quickly but had to wait for his wife. How interesting to read that the chief began seeking Coillard's advice only after he was engaged to Christina. Then, when she came, her coming was praised as the arrival of "[their] mother and the mother of [their] wives."

This illustrates that, whereas single missionaries tend to have more flexibility and influence with students and other singles, married missionaries tend to have greater stability and more influence with families and churches, thus impacting larger segments of society.

Coillard's beard reminded me of my own experience. In the 1990s, Albanian men in my city typically wore suit jackets and sometimes ties around town. Even painters, construction workers, and plumbers would ride their bikes to their jobs dressed semi-formally, then change clothes on the site. Men were never seen in shorts, despite the intense summer heat and lack of air conditioning. Being 22 years old, unmarried, and planting churches in a society that respected age, I tried to dress like a 50-year old. But no matter how much I tried to compensate for my age, I was still young and single, and this presented as many obstacles as it did opportunities. For example, a few local men offered me their daughters, according to their customs, creating awkward moments. My missions courses in college had not addressed this! I tried to respond in culturally appropriate ways, without offending.

Experiences like these were building objective arguments for the superiority of married missions ministry. Even a die-hard celibate like David Livingstone ended up changing his mind—the man who went to the field with such an outspoken aversion to marriage and an almost self-aggrandizing commitment to being like the great apostle Paul or David Brainerd. As Belle Brain has shown us, for him it only took the right girl (and the right lion) to cure him of his dogmatism on the matter.

With tender episodes, Belle has reminded us that, at its core, marriage is a covenant of companionship and fellowship in a mission of eternal joy. Because of the book's brevity, however, and its focus on the missionaries' courtships, we are not offered much information about their marriages. My friend Matt, a married missionary in a difficult field, observed:

> The one thing that I feel is left out of the book is the sense that these were real husbands and wives who inevitably must have had struggles in their marriages. There is a sense of the idyllic and heroic in the book, post-marriage. In such strong individuals, I imagine there must have also been times of difficulty even in such clearly matched teams.

Well put! Despite this omission, however, the author does offer a sobering view of the cost of marriage and missions. Perhaps nothing in Christian history highlights this better than Adoniram Judson's honesty with Ann and his epic letter to her father about the trials she would face. Adoniram needed to know that Ann Hasseltine and her parents had full disclosure before they agreed to the joint venture. Remember, American missions to foreign lands was a brand new enterprise, so Adoniram presented the worst potential scenarios. Some think his letter to Mr. Hasseltine was over-dramatic. Maybe. But it was honorable. He wanted his future wife to make an *informed* decision. In the end, the couple and their parents did the math and concluded, "How short is time, how boundless is eternity!" The movements they pioneered still bear fruit.

Missionaries in love and married couples contemplating missions should consider the cost as seriously as Adoniram and Ann did—*before* committing to it. No amount of cost-counting, however, and no amount of training in cross-cultural ministry can *fully* prepare us for what we will face, whether leaving home for a third-world country or even a more modern country. I think Mike Tyson articulated this best (yes, the boxer, of all people). He said, "Everyone has a plan until they get punched in the face." I don't think I've ever met a missionary who at some point did not feel punched in the face by the enemy, or even below the belt by a friend. In time I learned how common it is for missionaries to struggle with the very fact that they are struggling. The enemy, when he is given opportunity, will even attack the marriage itself. I appreciate the resources available and the efforts of missions boards and counseling centers to offer help and debriefing to those who serve.

Let me conclude with gratitude for how the author has honored the parents of these missionaries. To me, parents are the unsung heroes of missions, past and present. They offer their precious little lambs to the Lord without fanfare or recognition. The love of parents—especially that of a mother—cannot be quantified, but like Mary, they feel a sword piercing their own souls whenever their children and grand-children say good-bye and board those airplanes.

Robert Moffat wrote to his in-laws, "I will never forget the sacrifice you have made in committing to His care your only daughter."

Nor should we.

My parents-in-law often told people how they loved missions, committing more and more dollars every year. My parents did this, too.

That did not hurt, they would say.

Then my father-in-law left his business career to assist one of the largest missionary organizations in the world. To do it, he and my mother-in-law had to give up a comfortable salary and a secure retirement. Even that did not hurt, they recall. It did not feel like a great sacrifice.

Then God called their daughter to the field.

That hurt, but they gave her with joy, just as my parents had offered me, finding strength in their fellowship with the Father who so loved the world that He gave His only begotten Son, that whosoever believes in Him should not perish, but have eternal life.

Made in the USA
Monee, IL
02 February 2023

26940637R00067